Earth's
Amazing
Environments

Elizabeth Corfe

Contents

Amazing Environments

Earth is home to many amazing environments.
Life is found nearly everywhere in these
environments – in deserts, oceans, tropical
rainforests and at the **poles**.

*a herd of camels in
the Judea desert*

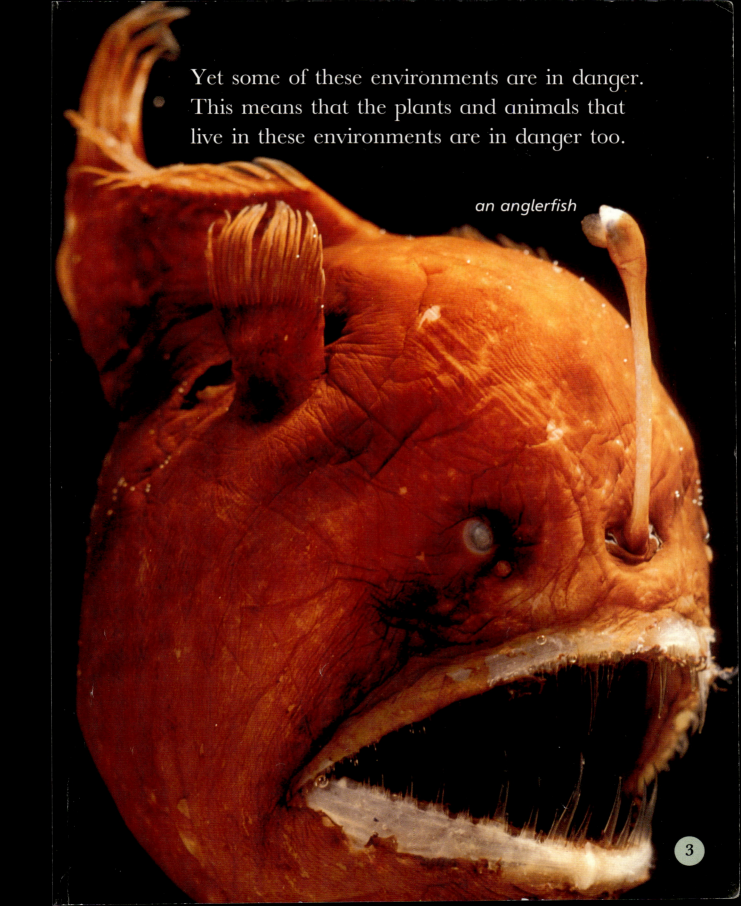

Yet some of these environments are in danger. This means that the plants and animals that live in these environments are in danger too.

an anglerfish

One cause of this danger is **global warming**. Global warming means Earth is getting hotter. It is caused by too many **greenhouse gases** in Earth's **atmosphere**.

Global warming has happened because of things such as:

- too much **pollution**, from cars and factories

- cutting down too many forests.

Global warming is bad for us and for the animals and plants we share Earth with.

Read on to learn about Earth's amazing environments, why they are in danger – and what **you** can do to help.

Deserts

Deserts are the driest environments on Earth. It hardly ever rains in a desert and a desert can be hot or cold.

Antarctic desert

The word *desert* comes from the Latin word *desertum* which means "an **abandoned** place".

Earth's Deserts

There are ten large deserts on Earth.

Sahara desert

Desert Life

In hot deserts the sun is strong, and the ground is hot.
These deserts seem empty … but are they?
Most hot deserts are full of life.

When the sun goes down,
a hot desert can get very cold.
Some can be 45°C in the day
and drop to 0°C at night!

a scorpion

During the day, most desert animals hide from the sun.
But as the sun goes down, the desert animals begin to stir.

Precious Water

Living things need water to **survive**.
Desert animals have to be clever
at getting and storing water.

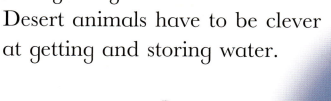

The Thorny Devil lizard stores
water in its thorns and skin.

The Fennec fox gets enough water
from the flesh of the animals it eats.

A camel stores fat in its hump.
The fat contains water.

Deserts in Danger

Global warming is putting Earth's deserts in danger. Some deserts are now hotter and drier than they should be.

With less water, desert plants and animals will no longer survive. Many may become **endangered** or even **extinct**.

a giraffe and ostriches looking for water

Oceans

Oceans cover around 70% of Earth's **surface**.

Oceans cover more than half of Earth.

Earth's Oceans

There are five large oceans on Earth.

the Pacific Ocean

Ocean Life

Plants and animals of all shapes, sizes and colours live in the ocean. Even the deepest, darkest and coldest parts of Earth's oceans have life.

This is a leafy sea dragon.
It looks like seaweed.

This is a Colossal squid.
They can grow to
around 14 metres long!

This is a blue whale.
It is the largest
animal on Earth!

This is an anglerfish.
It lives at the bottom
of the ocean.

Oceans in Danger

Global warming is making the oceans warmer, harming and even killing **marine** life.

Coral reefs are in danger because the coral will die if the ocean is too warm.

This coral, on the Great Barrier Reef in Australia, has died and turned white due to the ocean being too warm.

Marine animals such as whales will lose their food **supply**. Whales eat krill, and krill eat smaller ocean animals that may die due to global warming. So the krill will have no food, and the whales will have no food when the krill have gone.

a grey whale eating krill

Pollution such as oil spills can also kill marine life.

a bird covered in oil from an oil spill

Tropical Rainforests

Tropical rainforests are very wet, warm forests.
More than half of Earth's animal and plant **species**
live there.

The Amazon rainforest is the world's largest tropical rainforest.

Earth's Tropical Rainforests

Earth's main tropical rainforests are found near the **equator**.

Tropical rainforests

Chocolate, bananas and mangos all first grew in tropical rainforests.

Rainforest Life

The rainforest is filled with the sounds of animal, insect and bird life.

Colourful, beautiful and strange animals
live in tropical rainforests.

The Queen Alexandra butterfly
is the world's largest butterfly.
It lives in Papua New Guinea.

The orang-utan
lives in treetops
in Sumatra and
Borneo.

Rainforests in Danger

Global warming also harms rainforest plants and animals. As Earth becomes warmer and drier, parts of a rainforest may die. Many rainforest animals will no longer have a place to live.

The Sumatran orang-utan is very endangered. Many places where it lives have been destroyed by logging.

Earth's rainforests are also cut down for **logging**, **mining** and farming. This destroys many animals' **habitats**. Large numbers of rainforest animals have become endangered or extinct as a result.

In around 20 years time, over half of the Amazon rainforest will be gone. This is due to logging and clearing land for farming.

The Poles

The Poles are two large icy deserts. The Arctic is a huge area of ice covering the ocean around the North Pole. Antarctica is a huge area of ice that covers land around the South Pole.

a photo of Antarctica
taken from space

The Arctic and Antarctica

The Arctic is in the northern **hemisphere**.
Antarctica is in the southern hemisphere.

Antarctica

South Pole

North Pole

Arctic

The North Pole is the northernmost point on Earth. The South Pole is the southernmost point on Earth.

Life on the Ice

Animals live in the Arctic and Antarctica. Most of the animals that live there have thick layers of fur, feathers or fat called blubber. Blubber keeps the animals warm.

Emperor Penguins, Antarctica

Polar bears live in the Arctic. They have thick fur and blubber to survive the cold. They **hibernate** during the really freezing weather.

Emperor Penguins live in Antarctica. They have feathers and blubber to survive the cold. They also huddle together to keep warm.

Seals live in both **polar regions**. They have fur and thick blubber to survive the cold. They also hold their flippers against their bodies to keep warm.

a fur seal, Antarctica

Poles in Danger

Global warming is melting the ice in both the Arctic and Antarctica. Melting ice means animals that live in these environments will lose their habitats and **feeding grounds**.

Some scientists believe that within 100 years the polar bear will be extinct due to global warming.

Melting ice also means that ocean levels will rise, and may flood coastlines all over the world.

Adelie penguins, Antarctica

You Can Make a Difference!

Here are five things you can do to help protect Earth's amazing environments.

Action!	Why it Helps
recycling	• causes less pollution. • will slow down global warming.
saving water	• because all living things need water to survive.
using less electricity	• causes less pollution. • will slow down global warming.
walking	• walking more and driving less means less pollution will be released into the air. • will slow down global warming.
talking!	• spread the word about how to protect Earth's amazing environments.

Glossary

abandoned
left empty; not lived in

atmosphere
gases surrounding Earth

endangered
when a species is in danger of
becoming extinct

equator
imaginary line around the
middle of Earth

extinct
when a species dies out

feeding grounds
places on land or in water where
animals find food

global warming
heating up of Earth caused
by greenhouse gases

greenhouse gases
polluting gases that trap heat in
Earth's atmosphere

habitats
environments that animals
and plants live in

hemisphere
half of a sphere; Earth is a sphere so
has two hemispheres, the Northern
hemisphere and the Southern
hemisphere

hibernate
pass the winter in an almost
sleep-like state

logging
cutting down trees

marine
to do with the ocean

mining
digging in the earth for things
such as coal

polar regions
areas on Earth known as the poles

pollution
dangerous or dirty substances in
the air, water, or land

species
group of animals or plants that
are alike

surface
top, or outer, layer of something

survive
live

supply
goods, amounts of something

Index